Australia

Helen Arnold

RSVP
**RAINTREE
STECK-VAUGHN**
P U B L I S H E R S
The Steck-Vaughn Company

Austin, Texas

Published by Raintree Steck-Vaughn Publishers, an imprint of Steck-Vaughn Company

A ZOË BOOK

Editor: Kath Davies, Helene Resky
Design: Jan Sterling, Sterling Associates
Map: Gecko Limited
Production: Grahame Griffiths

Library of Congress Cataloging-in-Publication Data

Arnold, Helen.
    Australia / Helen Arnold.
        p. cm. — (Postcards from)
    Includes index.
    ISBN 0-8172-4010-1 (lib. binding)
    ISBN 0-8172-4231-7 (softcover)
    1. Australia — Description and travel — Juvenile literature.
    [1. Australia — Description and travel. 2. Letters.] I. Title. II. Series.
    DU105.2.A76 1996
    944–dc20   95–15225
                                                                    CIP
                                                                    AC

Printed and bound in the United States
    4 5 6 7 8 9 0 WZ 99

Photographic acknowledgments

The publishers wish to acknowledge, with thanks, the following photographic sources:

The Hutchison Library / Hilly Janes - title page, 12, 14; Robert Harding Picture Library / Margaret Collier 10; Impact Photos / Neil Morrison - cover bl, 24; / John Miles 20; / Sally Fear 28; Zefa - cover tl & r, 6, 8, 16, 18, 22, 26.

The publishers have made every effort to trace the copyright holders, but if they have inadvertently overlooked any, they will be pleased to make the necessary arrangement at the first opportunity.

Contents

All the words that appear in **bold** are explained in the Glossary on page 30.

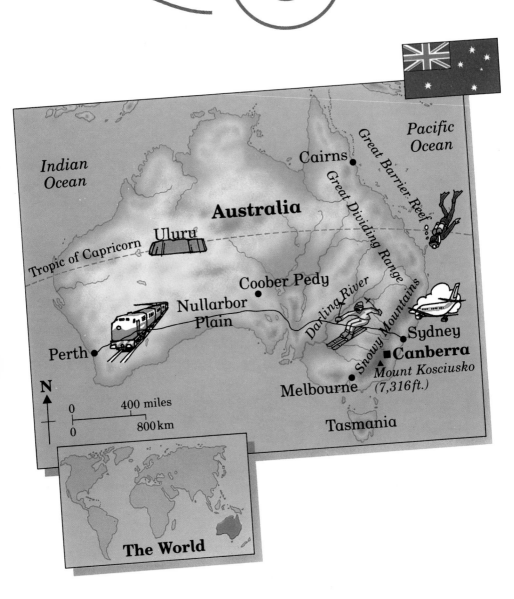

A big map of Australia
and a small map of the world

Dear Martina,

It took almost a whole day and night to fly to Australia. It is on the other side of the world from the United States. You can see Australia in red on the small map. It is the biggest island in the world.

Love,

Patsy

P.S. Mom says that Australia is almost as big as the United States. Australia is a **continent** as well as a country.

A bird's eye view of Sydney

Dear Eric,

Today we went on a boat across Sydney harbor. Sydney is the biggest city in Australia. We are going shopping now. I have some Australian money. It is called dollars.

Your friend,

Paul

P.S. Dad says there are far fewer people living in Australia than in the United States. Most people in Australia live in towns or cities near the ocean. Canberra is the **capital** city. It is smaller than Sydney.

Streetcars in the middle of Melbourne

Dear Sophie,

We caught a **streetcar** like this one in Melbourne. People in Australia speak English, but we heard some people speaking Greek on the streetcar. We had Greek food for dinner last night. I liked it.

Your friend,

Craig

P.S. Mom says that people came from all over the world to live in Australia. Many people who live in Melbourne came from Greece and Italy.

The Australian high-speed train, the XPT

Dear Shane,

I want to go on a train like this one. Most places in Australia are a long way from each other. People usually fly from city to city. It is the quickest way to travel around.

Yours,

Bobby

P.S. Uncle Jack says that the XPT train takes three days to go from Sydney to Perth. The railroad line is straight for about 300 miles (480 km) across Nullarbor Plain.

A cattle station in the outback

Dear Susan,

We are almost in the middle of Australia now. It is very hot and dry here. The country is called the **outback**. We have seen lots of sheep and some cattle. They are kept on large farms called **stations**.

Love,

Ronnie

P.S. Uncle David says that his station is almost as big as Massachusetts! Some of the dry land is **desert**.

13

Shearing sheep

Dear Carlos,

The sheep **shearers** work very fast. They cut the wool off a sheep in one piece. The wool is called a **fleece**. They are careful, so the sheep is not hurt. I bet the sheep feels cold for a while!

Your friend,

Alex

P.S. Mom says that more than a quarter of all the wool in the world comes from Australia. A lot of lamb and beef comes from Australia, too.

A kangaroo in the outback

Dear Lauren,

Australia is the only place in the world where wild kangaroos live. At last I have seen some. They are much bigger than I am. They take big jumps, so they move fast through the outback.

See you soon,

Claire

P.S. Dad says that many wild animals and plants are found only in Australia. I want to see a **koala**. Koalas live in the country called the **bush**.

Uluru, also called Ayers Rock

Dear Phil,

This big red rock is almost in the middle of Australia. The people who first lived in Australia are called **Aborigines**. They call the rock Uluru. It is a special place for them.

Yours,

Darren

P.S. Mom says that the Aborigines have lived in Australia for thousands of years. People from Europe first settled here about 200 years ago.

A special house at Coober Pedy

Dear Kelly,

We came to see a house like this one. It is in a cave under the ground. Some **tourists** come to Coober Pedy to buy **opals**. These stones are beautiful colors.

Love,

Denise

P.S. Dad says that people who mined made the caves to live in when they first came to dig for opals. The name *Coober Pedy* comes from the Aboriginal language. It means "white man in a hole."

Skiing in the Snowy Mountains

Dear Joe,

We are skiing in the high Snowy Mountains. Some families take a short winter vacation here. I know it is summer in the United States now, but in Australia it is winter!

Your friend,

Max

P.S. Mom says that the seasons are different because Australia is on the other side of the Earth from the United States.

Bondi Beach, Sydney

Dear Julie,

This is one of the most famous beaches in Australia. It is very crowded on the weekends. The Australians love swimming. They are good at many sports.

Love,

Lisa

P.S. It is very hot here in summer. Aunt Joan says we have to "slip, slop, slap." This stands for, slip on a T-shirt, slop on some sunscreen, and slap on a hat!

A blue-girdled angelfish

Dear Jimmy,

This fish lives in the Great Barrier **Reef**. The reef is made of **coral**. It is more than 1,000 miles (1,600 km) long. We went out in a boat that had a glass bottom. We could see the fish under the water.

Yours,

Stewart

P.S. Mom says that about 1,500 different kinds of fish live in the reef. I would like to see all of them!

Children holding Australian flags

Dear Sue,

The stars on the Australian flag look like stars called the Southern Cross. You can see these stars in the sky when you are south of the **equator**.

Love,

Rachael

P.S. Can you see the British flag on the Australian flag? Dad says that Great Britain once ruled Australia. Now the people choose their own rulers. Australia is a **democracy**.

Glossary

Aborigines: The first people to live in Australia

Bush: The name for the area in Australia that has trees and woods

Capital: The town or city where people who rule the country meet

Continent: One of the seven main, large pieces of land in the world

Coral: Red, white, or pink rock made of the dead bodies of tiny sea animals

Democracy: A country where the people choose the leaders they want to run the country

Desert: A place where there is very little water or rain. Very few plants or animals can live there.

Equator: The line drawn on maps to show the middle of the Earth

Fleece: A coat of wool

Koala: A furry animal that looks like a bear

Opal: A colored stone worth a lot of money

Outback: The dry lands and deserts in the middle of Australia, where few trees can grow

P.S.: This stands for Post Script. A postscript is the part of a card or letter that is added at the end, after the person has signed it.

Reef: A line of rocks or coral close to the surface of the ocean

Shearer: Someone who cuts the wool off sheep

Station: A ranch

Streetcar: A train that runs on the street

Tourist: A person who is taking a vacation away from home

Index